more CUTE LITTLE ANiMALS
to crochet

There's a whole world of stuff happening in this animal kingdom—and it may surprise you!

These crocheted critters are lively little folk. They have jobs. They have friends. And they have adventures! That's because they're amigurumi, crocheted dolls inspired by the Japanese craft trend. Amy Gaines is the creative force behind Purl, the online pattern company that introduced crocheters and knitters around the world to Amy's friendly yarn-based life forms.

Want to meet 8 more of Amy's fun critters in crochet? Visit leisurearts.com to buy leaflet #4271 Cute Little Animals. You'll make the acquaintance of the Loch Ness monster, a pirate panda, a sweet pup, a memorable elephant, a larcenous cat, and three other fun, fanciful dolls.

LEISURE ARTS, INC.
Little Rock, Arkansas

thoReau

See that little gnome there? That's Thoreau. In the realm of magical folk, he's an attorney, but his real passion is hybridizing mushrooms. He used to live in the Oak Woods, where he grew a garden of tasty red fungi. The chipmunks living nearby couldn't resist stealing the little morsels. Since chipmunks aren't magical (or very bright), the only option available to Thoreau was to open his Faery Book of Law and "read" these words aloud: "Red mushrooms belong to Thoreau. All other mushrooms belong to everyone else." But the chipmunks helped themselves to the mushrooms anyway. Finally, Thoreau arose early one day, gathered his mushrooms into a tote bag, and walked across the valley to Farmer Jones's Dairy. After Jones got over his surprise at meeting an actual gnome, he listened to Thoreau's business proposition. And that's how Thoreau became a partner in the mushroom biz. He grows the little treats in an old hay barn while Jones sells them by the pound. Just for old time's sake, the gnome sometimes "reads" to the timid barn mice: "All mushrooms belong to Jones-Thoreau, Inc. Corporate shares are available for purchase. Inquiries welcome."

Finished Size: 8½" (21.5 cm) tall

MATERIALS
Medium Weight Yarn **(4)** MEDIUM
[3 ounces, 157 yards
(85 grams, 144 meters) per skein]:
 Tan - 1 skein
[3.5 ounces, 190 yards
(99 grams, 174 meters) per skein]:
 White, Red, Black, Brown, Blue, **and** Green
 - 1 skein **each** color
 Yellow - small amount
Crochet hook, size G (4 mm) **or** size needed
 for gauge
6 mm Doll eyes - 2
Polyester fiberfill
Stuffing pellets
Felt - small piece of pink for cheeks and
 tan for belt buckle
Embroidery floss - small amount of pink and
 tan
Sewing needle
Yarn needle

GAUGE: 16 sc and 18 rows/rnds = 4" (10 cm)

Gauge Swatch: 4" (10 cm) square
Ch 17.
Row 1: Sc in second ch from hook and in each ch
across: 16 sc.
Rows 2-18: Ch 1, turn; sc in each sc across.
Finish off.

STITCH GUIDE
● **DECREASE**
● Pull up a loop in next 2 sc, YO and draw
● through all 3 loops on hook (**counts as one sc**).

THOREAU
HEAD
Rnd 1 (Right side)**:** With Tan, ch 2; 6 sc in second ch from hook; do **not** join, place marker to mark beginning of rnd (*see Markers, page 42*).

Rnd 2: 2 Sc in each sc around: 12 sc.

Rnd 3: (2 Sc in next sc, sc in next sc) around: 18 sc.

Rnd 4: (2 Sc in next sc, sc in next 2 sc) around: 24 sc.

Rnd 5: (2 Sc in next sc, sc in next 3 sc) around: 30 sc.

Rnds 6-8: Sc in each sc around.

Rnd 9: Sc in next 14 sc, 2 sc in each of next 2 sc (nose), sc in next 14 sc: 32 sc.

Rnd 10: Sc in next 14 sc, 2 sc in each of next 4 sc, sc in next 14 sc: 36 sc.

Rnd 11: Sc in next 14 sc, decrease 4 times, sc in next 14 sc: 32 sc.

Rnd 12: Sc in next 14 sc, decrease twice, sc in next 14 sc: 30 sc.

Rnd 13: (Decrease, sc in next 3 sc) around: 24 sc.

Rnd 14: (Decrease, sc in next 2 sc) around; slip st in next sc, finish off leaving a long end for sewing: 18 sc.

Using photo as a guide, page 2, attach eyes to Head on Rnd 8.

Cut two ½" (12 mm) circles from pink felt for cheeks.
Using photo as a guide and a single strand of pink floss, sew cheeks to Head.
Stuff Head firmly with fiberfill.

BEARD
With White, ch 15.

Row 1 (Right side): Sc in second ch from hook and in next 2 chs, hdc in next ch, 2 hdc in next ch, 2 dc in each of next 4 chs, 2 hdc in next ch, hdc in next ch, sc in last 3 chs; finish off leaving a long end for sewing: 20 sts.

 Note Loop a short piece of yarn around any stitch to mark Row 1 as **right** side.

Using photo as a guide, sew Beard to Head.

HAT
Rnd 1 (Right side): With Red, ch 2; 4 sc in second ch from hook; do **not** join, place marker to mark beginning of rnd.

Rnd 2: Sc in each sc around.

Rnd 3: 2 Sc in each sc around: 8 sc.

Rnd 4: Sc in each sc around.

Rnd 5: (2 Sc in next sc, sc in next sc) around: 12 sc.

Rnd 6: Sc in each sc around.

Rnd 7: (2 Sc in next sc, sc in next 2 sc) around: 16 sc.

Rnd 8: Sc in each sc around.

Rnd 9: (2 Sc in next sc, sc in next 3 sc) around: 20 sc.

Rnd 10: Sc in each sc around.

Rnd 11: (2 Sc in next sc, sc in next 4 sc) around: 24 sc.

Rnd 12: Sc in each sc around.

Rnd 13: (2 Sc in next sc, sc in next 5 sc) around: 28 sc.

Rnd 14: Sc in each sc around.

Rnd 15: (2 Sc in next sc, sc in next 6 sc) around: 32 sc.

Rnd 16: Sc in each sc around; slip st in next sc, finish off leaving a long end for sewing.

Stuff Hat lightly with fiberfill.
Using photo as a guide, sew Hat to Head covering ends of Beard.

Instructions continued on page 6.

EAR (Make 2)

Rnd 1 (Right side): With Tan, ch 2; 6 sc in second ch from hook; do **not** join, place marker to mark beginning of rnd.

Rnd 2: (2 Sc in next sc, sc in next 2 sc) twice; slip st in next sc, finish off leaving a long end for sewing: 8 sc.

Thread yarn needle with long end. Beginning at slip st, fold Ear with **wrong** side together. Matching sts on Rnd 2 and working through **both** thicknesses, sew Ear closed. Using photo as a guide, sew folded edge of Ears to Head below Hat edge and behind Beard.

BODY

Rnd 1 (Right side): With Black, ch 2; 6 sc in second ch from hook; do **not** join, place marker to mark beginning of rnd.

Rnd 2: 2 Sc in each sc around: 12 sc.

Rnd 3: (2 Sc in next sc, sc in next sc) around: 18 sc.

Rnd 4: (2 Sc in next sc, sc in next 2 sc) around: 24 sc.

Rnd 5: (2 Sc in next sc, sc in next 3 sc) around: 30 sc.

Rnd 6: (2 Sc in next sc, sc in next 4 sc) around: 36 sc.

Rnds 7 and 8: Sc in each sc around.

Rnd 9: Sc in each sc around changing to Brown in last sc made (*Fig. 2, page 42*).

Rnds 10 and 11: Sc in each sc around.

Rnd 12: Sc in each sc around changing to Blue in last sc made.

Rnds 13 and 14: Sc in each sc around.

Rnd 15: (Decrease, sc in next 4 sc) around: 30 sc.

Rnd 16: (Decrease, sc in next 3 sc) around: 24 sc.

Rnd 17: (Decrease, sc in next 2 sc) around; slip st in next sc, finish off leaving a long end for sewing: 18 sc.

Cut one belt buckle from tan felt.

BELT BUCKLE PATTERN

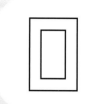

Using photo as a guide and a single strand of tan floss, sew belt buckle to Body.

Fill half the Body with pellets, then stuff remaining Body with fiberfill. Thread yarn needle with long end on Head. Matching sts on last rnd of Head to last rnd of Body, sew Head to Body.

ARM (Make 2)

Rnd 1 (Right side): With Tan, ch 2; 4 sc in second ch from hook; do **not** join, place marker to mark beginning of rnd.

Rnd 2: 2 Sc in each sc around: 8 sc.

Rnd 3: Sc in each sc around.

Rnd 4: Sc in each sc around changing to Blue in last sc made.

Rnds 5-8: Sc in each sc around.

Rnd 9: Sc in each sc around; slip st in next sc, finish off leaving a long end for sewing.

Stuff bottom of Arm lightly with fiberfill. Beginning at slip st, flatten Rnd 9. Using photo as a guide and working through all thicknesses, sew Arms to Rnd 17 on Body.

MUSHROOM

Rnd 1 (Right side): With White, ch 2; 6 sc in second ch from hook; do **not** join, place marker to mark beginning of rnd (*see Markers, page 42*).

Rnd 2: 2 Sc in each sc around: 12 sc.

Rnd 3: Sc in Back Loop Only of each sc around (*Fig. 1, page 42*).

Rnd 4: Sc in both loops of each sc around.

Rnd 5: Sc in each sc around changing to Red in last sc made (*Fig. 2, page 42*).

Rnd 6: (2 Sc in next sc, sc in next sc) around: 18 sc.

Rnd 7: (2 Sc in next sc, sc in next 2 sc) around: 24 sc.

Rnd 8: Sc in Back Loop Only of each sc around.

Rnds 9 and 10: Sc in both loops of each sc around.

Rnd 11: (Decrease, sc in next 2 sc) around: 18 sc.

Stuff Mushroom firmly with fiberfill.

Rnd 12: (Decrease, sc in next sc) around: 12 sc.

Rnd 13: Decrease around; slip st in next sc, finish off leaving a long end for sewing: 6 sc.

Thread yarn needle with long end, weave needle through sc on Rnd 13; gather **tightly** to close and secure end.

LARGE SPOT

Rnd 1 (Right side): With White, ch 2; 6 sc in second ch from hook; do **not** join, place marker to mark beginning of rnd.

Rnd 2: 2 Sc in each sc around; slip st in next sc, finish off leaving a long end for sewing: 12 sc.

SMALL SPOT (Make 2)

Rnd 1 (Right side): With White, ch 2; 6 sc in second ch from hook; join with slip st to first sc, finish off leaving a long end for sewing.

Using photos as a guide, sew Spots to Mushroom.

LAWN

Rnd 1 (Right side): With Green, ch 2; 6 sc in second ch from hook; do **not** join, place marker to mark beginning of rnd (*see Markers, page 42*).

Rnd 2: 2 Sc in each sc around: 12 sc.

Rnd 3: (2 Sc in next sc, sc in next sc) around: 18 sc.

Rnd 4: (2 Sc in next sc, sc in next 2 sc) around: 24 sc.

Rnd 5: (2 Sc in next sc, sc in next 3 sc) around: 30 sc.

Rnd 6: (2 Sc in next sc, sc in next 4 sc) around: 36 sc.

Rnd 7: (2 Sc in next sc, sc in next 5 sc) around: 42 sc.

Rnd 8: (2 Sc in next sc, sc in next 6 sc) around; slip st in next sc, finish off: 48 sc.

FLOWER

Rnd 1 (Right side): With Yellow, ch 2; 5 sc in second ch from hook; do **not** join, place marker to mark beginning of rnd (*see Markers, page 42*).

Rnd 2: (2 Hdc, slip st) in each sc around; slip st in next hdc, finish off leaving a long end for sewing.

Using Red and straight stitch (*Fig. 6, page 43*), work an "X" in center of Flower.

All pieces may be left separate or sewn to the Lawn.

beAtrix

If you've ever dreamed of taking art lessons but haven't shown any aptitude beyond the pages of a coloring book, you should contact Ms. Beatrix Hedgehog. She loves to teach. She has an MA in Fine Art and all the patience in the world. Just don't be surprised if it takes a while for her to answer the door on your first visit. Like most hedgehogs, she has a tendency to roll up in a ball when feeling timid. She's seeing a therapist about it, but innate impulses are difficult to overcome. If you have no interest in art, you may still be interested to know that Beatrix is a wiz with barber's scissors and hair dye. One can only suppose her interest in hairstyling grew out of having quills that can't be curled or colored at all. And believe us, Beatrix has tried. There was an incident with purple dye...well, we better leave that for Beatrix to tell. You'll find her studio/salon above the Hoot, Hoot, Whooray! Café. Take the stairs at the back of the building and be careful not to peek into the café windows as you go by— unless you really, really want a cup of herbal coffee and a goat cheese croissant.

Finished Size: 4¹/₂" (11.5 cm) tall

MATERIALS
Medium Weight Yarn **④**
  [3.5 ounces, 170 yards
  (100 grams, 156 meters) per skein]:
    Ecru **and** Brown -
      1 skein **each** color **⑤**
Bulky Weight Novelty Yarn
  [1.75 ounces, 64 yards
  (50 grams, 58 meters) per skein]:
    Brown - 1 skein
Crochet hook, size G (4 mm) **or** size needed
  for gauge
6 mm Doll eyes - 2
Polyester fiberfill
Yarn needle
Safety pin

GAUGE: 16 sc and 18 rows/rnds = 4" (10 cm)

Gauge Swatch: 4" (10 cm) square
Ch 17.
Row 1: Sc in second ch from hook and in each ch across: 16 sc.
Rows 2-18: Ch 1, turn; sc in each sc across. Finish off.

STITCH GUIDE
● **DECREASE**
● Pull up a loop in next 2 sc, YO and draw
● through all 3 loops on hook (**counts as one sc**).

BEATRIX
HEAD
Rnd 1 (Right side)**:** With Ecru, ch 2; 6 sc in second ch from hook; do **not** join, place marker to mark beginning of rnd (**see Markers, page 42**).

Rnd 2: 2 Sc in each sc around: 12 sc.

Rnd 3: (2 Sc in next sc, sc in next sc) around: 18 sc.

Rnd 4: Sc in each sc around.

Rnd 5: Sc in next 8 sc, 2 sc in each of next 2 sc (muzzle), sc in next 8 sc: 20 sc.

Rnd 6: Sc in next 9 sc, 2 sc in each of next 2 sc, sc in next 9 sc: 22 sc.

Rnd 7: Sc in next 10 sc, 2 sc in each of next 2 sc, sc in next 10 sc: 24 sc.

Rnd 8: Sc in next 11 sc, 2 sc in each of next 2 sc, sc in next 11 sc: 26 sc.

Rnd 9: Sc in next 9 sc, decrease 4 times, sc in next 9 sc: 22 sc.

Rnd 10: Sc in next 7 sc, decrease 4 times, sc in next 7 sc: 18 sc.

Slip loop from hook onto safety pin to prevent work from unraveling while attaching eyes. Using photo as a guide, page 11, attach eyes to Head on Rnd 6.

BODY
Rnd 1: Slip loop from safety pin onto hook; (2 sc in next sc, sc in next 2 sc) around: 24 sc.

Rnds 2-9: Sc in each sc around.

Rnd 10: (Decrease, sc in next 2 sc) around: 18 sc.

Rnd 11: (Decrease, sc in next sc) around: 12 sc.

Stuff Head and Body firmly with fiberfill.

Rnd 12: Decrease around; slip st in next sc, finish off leaving a long end for sewing: 6 sc.

Thread needle with long end, weave needle through sc on Rnd 12; gather **tightly** to close and secure end.

SPIKES
Rnd 1 (Right side): Holding one strand of Brown medium weight yarn and one strand of Brown novelty yarn together, ch 2; 6 sc second ch from hook; do **not** join, place marker to mark beginning of rnd.

Rnd 2: 2 Sc in each sc around: 12 sc.

Rnd 3: (2 Sc in next sc, sc in next sc) around: 18 sc.

Rnd 4: (2 Sc in next sc, sc in next 2 sc) around: 24 sc.

Rnd 5: (2 Sc in next sc, sc in next 3 sc) around: 30 sc.

Rnds 6-8: Sc in each sc around.

Rnd 9: Sc in each sc around; slip st in next sc, finish off leaving a long end for sewing.

Beginning at slip st, flatten Rnd 9. Using photo as a guide and working through all thicknesses, sew Spikes to back of Head and Body.

NOSE
Rnd 1 (Right side): With Brown medium weight yarn, ch 2; 6 sc in second ch from hook; do **not** join, place marker to mark beginning of rnd.

Rnd 2: Sc in each sc around; slip st in next sc, finish off leaving a long end for sewing.

Using photo as a guide, sew Nose to muzzle on Head.

LEG (Make 4)
Rnd 1 (Right side): With Ecru, ch 2; 6 sc in second ch from hook; do **not** join, place marker to mark beginning of rnd.

Rnd 2: Sc in each sc around.

Rnd 3: Sc in each sc around; slip st in next sc, finish off leaving a long end for sewing.

Beginning at slip st, flatten Rnd 3. Using photo as a guide and working through all thicknesses, sew two Legs to upper Body at neck and two Legs to bottom of Body.

hEdda & SYblE

With their wide-eyed interest in any subject you can name, Hedda Ooglesby and teen daughter Syble are the best conversationalists in town. These are the go-to owl gals, whether you want to talk about local politics, world events, or just share some friendly gossip. They're also fantastic salespersons, serving up organic foods in their Hoot, Hoot, Whooray! Café. The regular customers who dine on sunflower seed biscuits with yak butter claim that the popularity of the place is all about its cozy atmosphere. But there are those who think the café's success has more to do with Hedda being something of an amateur mesmerist. They say if you look into her big glowing eyes while she speaks of whatever is dear to your heart, you'll find yourself agreeing to a second cup of coffee and an extra guava-kiwi-date-nut muffin. Ask her about her rumored talent and Hedda will hoot so charmingly that you'll find yourself laughing along. Besides, those guava muffins really are pretty tasty!

Finished Sizes
Hedda - 5¼" (13.5 cm) tall
Syble - 4" (10 cm) tall

MATERIALS
Medium Weight Yarn
[3.5 ounces, 170 yards
(100 grams, 156 meters) per skein]:
Dk Brown, Brown, **and** Lt Brown - 1 skein
each color
White - small amount
Crochet hook, size G (4 mm) **or** size needed
for gauge
9 mm Doll eyes - 4
Polyester fiberfill
Yarn needle
Safety pin

GAUGE: 16 sc and 18 rows/rnds = 4" (10 cm)

Gauge Swatch: 4" (10 cm) square
Ch 17.
Row 1: Sc in second ch from hook and in each ch
across: 16 sc.
Rows 2-18: Ch 1, turn; sc in each sc across.
Finish off.

STITCH GUIDE
● **DECREASE**
● Pull up a loop in next 2 sts, YO and draw
● through all 3 loops on hook (**counts as**
● **one sc**).

HEDDA
EYE PATCH (Make 2)
Rnd 1 (Right side)**:** With White, ch 2; 6 sc in
second ch from hook; do **not** join, place marker to
mark beginning of rnd (*see Markers, page 42*).

Rnd 2: 2 Sc in each sc around: 12 sc.

Rnd 3: (2 Sc in next sc, sc in next sc) around; slip st
in next sc, finish off leaving a long end for sewing:
18 sc.

Thread needle with long end and sew 2 sc of each
Eye Patch together.

HEAD

Rnd 1 (Right side)**:** With Dk Brown, ch 2; 8 sc in second ch from hook; do **not** join, place marker to mark beginning of rnd.

Rnd 2: 2 Sc in each sc around: 16 sc.

Rnd 3: (2 Sc in next sc, sc in next sc) around: 24 sc.

Rnd 4: (2 Sc in next sc, sc in next 2 sc) around: 32 sc.

Rnds 5-10: Sc in each sc around.

Rnd 11: (Decrease, sc in next 2 sc) around changing to Brown in last sc made (*Fig. 2, page 42*): 24 sc.

BODY

Rnd 1: Sc in each sc around.

Slip loop from hook onto safety pin to prevent work from unraveling while attaching eyes. Using photo as a guide, page 13, insert an eye through center of each Eye Patch and attach to Head on Rnd 9.

Rnd 2: Slip loop from safety pin onto hook; (2 sc in next sc, sc in next 3 sc) around: 30 sc.

Rnds 3-13: Sc in each sc around.

Rnd 14: (Decrease, sc in next 3 sc) around: 24 sc.

Rnd 15: (Decrease, sc in next 2 sc) around: 18 sc.

Rnd 16: (Decrease, sc in next sc) around: 12 sc.

Stuff Head and Body firmly with fiberfill.

Rnd 17: Decrease around; slip st in next sc, finish off leaving a long end for sewing: 6 sc.

Thread needle with long end, weave needle through sc on Rnd 17; gather **tightly** to close and secure end.

WING (Make 2)

Rnd 1 (Right side)**:** With Dk Brown, ch 2; 6 sc in second ch from hook; do **not** join, place marker to mark beginning of rnd.

Rnd 2: 2 Sc in each sc around: 12 sc.

Rnd 3: (2 Sc in next sc, sc in next sc) around: 18 sc.

Rnds 4-10: Sc in each sc around.

Rnd 11: (Decrease, sc in next sc) around; slip st in next sc, finish off leaving a long end for sewing: 12 sc.

Beginning at slip st, flatten Rnd 11. Using photo as a guide and working through all thicknesses, sew Wings to Body on Rnd 1.

EAR (Make 2)

Rnd 1 (Right side)**:** With Dk Brown and leaving a long end for sewing, ch 2; 4 sc in second ch from hook; do **not** join, place marker to mark beginning of rnd.

Rnd 2: 2 Sc in each sc around: 8 sc.

Rnd 3: (2 Sc in next sc, sc in next sc) around; slip st in next sc, finish off: 12 sc.

Using photo as a guide, sew Ears to Head.

Instructions continued on page 16.

FOOT (Make 2)
Rnd 1 (Right side): With Lt Brown, ch 2; 6 sc in second ch from hook; do **not** join, place marker to mark beginning of rnd.

Rnd 2: 2 Sc in each sc around; slip st in next sc, finish off leaving a long end for sewing: 12 sc.

Thread needle with long end. Beginning at slip st, fold Foot with **wrong** side together. Matching sts on Rnd 2 and working through **both** thicknesses, sew Foot closed. Using photo as a guide, sew folded edge of Feet to bottom of Body.

BEAK
With Lt Brown, ch 5.

Row 1 (Right side): Sc in second from hook and in each ch across: 4 sc.

 Note Loop a short piece of yarn around any stitch to mark Row 1 as **right** side.

Row 2: Ch 1, turn; insert hook in first sc and in next sc, YO and draw through all 3 loops on hook (**counts as first sc**), decrease: 2 sc.

Row 3: Ch 1, turn; insert hook in first sc and in last sc, YO and draw through all 3 loops on hook (**counts as first sc**); finish off leaving a long end for sewing: one sc.

Using photo as a guide, sew Beak to Head.

SYBLE
EYE PATCH (Make 2)
Rnd 1 (Right side): With White, ch 2; 6 sc in second ch from hook; do **not** join, place marker to mark beginning of rnd (*see Markers, page 42*).

Rnd 2: 2 Sc in each sc around; slip st in next sc, finish off leaving a long end for sewing: 12 sc.

Thread needle with long end and sew one sc of each Eye Patch together.

HEAD
Rnd 1 (Right side): With Brown, ch 2; 8 sc in second ch from hook; do **not** join, place marker to mark beginning of rnd.

Rnd 2: 2 Sc in each sc around: 16 sc.

Rnd 3: (2 Sc in next sc, sc in next sc) around: 24 sc.

Rnds 4-7: Sc in each sc around.

Rnd 8: (Decrease, sc in next 2 sc) around changing to Lt Brown in last sc made: 18 sc.

BODY
Rnd 1: Sc in each sc around.

Slip loop from hook onto safety pin to prevent work from unraveling while attaching eyes. Using photo as a guide, page 13, insert an eye through center of each Eye Patch and attach to Head on Rnd 6.

Rnd 2: Slip loop from safety pin onto hook; (2 sc in next sc, sc in next 2 sc) around: 24 sc.

Rnds 3-9: Sc in each sc around.

Rnd 10: (Decrease, sc in next 2 sc) around: 18 sc.

Rnd 11: (Decrease, sc in next sc) around: 12 sc.

Stuff Head and Body firmly with fiberfill.

Rnd 12: Decrease around; slip st in next sc, finish off leaving a long end for sewing: 6 sc.

Thread needle with long end, weave needle through sc on Rnd 12; gather **tightly** to close and secure end.

WING (Make 2)

Rnd 1 (Right side): With Brown, ch 2; 6 sc in second ch from hook; do **not** join, place marker to mark beginning of rnd.

Rnd 2: 2 Sc in each sc around: 12 sc.

Rnds 3-7: Sc in each sc around.

Rnd 8: Decrease around; slip st in next sc, finish off leaving a long end for sewing: 6 sc.

Beginning at slip st, flatten Rnd 8. Using photo as a guide and working through all thicknesses, sew Wings to Head on Rnd 8.

EAR (Make 2)

Rnd 1 (Right side): With Brown and leaving a long end for sewing, ch 2; 3 sc in second ch from hook; do **not** join, place marker to mark beginning of rnd.

Rnd 2: 2 Sc in each sc around: 6 sc.

Rnd 3: (2 Sc in next sc, sc in next sc) around; slip st in next sc, finish off leaving a long end for sewing: 9 sc.

Using photo as a guide, sew Ears to Head on Rnds 3-5.

FOOT (Make 2)

Rnd 1 (Right side): With Dk Brown, ch 2; 8 sc in second ch from hook; join with slip st to first sc, finish off leaving a long end for sewing.

Thread needle with long end. Beginning at slip st, fold Foot with **wrong** side together. Matching sts on Rnd 1 and working through **both** thicknesses, sew Foot closed. Using photo as a guide, sew folded edge of Feet to bottom of Body.

BEAK

With Dk Brown, ch 5.

Row 1 (Right side): Insert hook in second ch from hook and in next ch, YO and draw through all 3 loops on hook (**counts as first sc**), decrease: 2 sc.

 Note Mark Row 1 as **right** side.

Row 2: Ch 1, turn; insert hook in first sc and in last sc, YO and draw through all 3 loops on hook (**counts as first sc**); finish off leaving a long end for sewing: one sc.

Using photo as a guide, sew Beak to Head.

frannie
FINCH

You've heard of boomerang kids—children who move out of their parents' home, then move back in a while later? That rarely happens with birds, except for poor Frannie Finch. It seems like she just gets one batch of fledglings out of the nest when the previous season's chicks come flying back. She's hoping this pair of little darlings will be a bit more independent. There is some good news to feed that hope. A huge subdivision is under construction nearby, and several new homeowners have already installed birdfeeders in their backyards. Frannie doesn't ordinarily believe in fast food, but if it will get her youngsters in the habit of looking elsewhere for their meals, she will happily set aside her concerns. Of course, she could just do what her cousin Frederica did last year—retire to Florida. Says the cousin, "Life as an empty-nester is 'tweet!'"

Finished Size: Approximately 13" (33 cm) height

MATERIALS
Medium Weight Yarn 🔵**4**
  [3.5 ounces, 190 yards
  (99 grams, 174 meters) per skein]:
    Dk Brown, Green, Brown, **and** Blue -
      1 skein **each** color
    Dk Green - small amount
Crochet hook, size G (4 mm) **or** size needed
  for gauge
6 mm Doll eyes - 6
Polyester fiberfill
1¼" (3 cm) Plastic ring
Heavy duty thread
Yarn needle
Safety pin

GAUGE: 16 sc and 18 rows/rnds = 4" (10 cm)

Gauge Swatch: 4" (10 cm) square
Ch 17.
Row 1: Sc in second ch from hook and in each ch
across: 16 sc.
Rows 2-18: Ch 1, turn; sc in each sc across.
Finish off.

STITCH GUIDE
● **DECREASE**
● Pull up a loop in next 2 sc, YO and draw
● through all 3 loops on hook (**counts as**
● **one sc**).

LOG
BODY
Rnd 1 (Right side): With Brown, ch 2; 6 sc in
second ch from hook; do **not** join, place marker to
mark beginning of rnd (*see Markers, page 42*).

Rnd 2: 2 Sc in each sc around: 12 sc.

Rnd 3: (2 Sc in next sc, sc in next sc) around: 18 sc.

Rnd 4: (2 Sc in next sc, sc in next 2 sc) around
changing to Dk Brown in last sc made (*Fig. 2,
page 42*): 24 sc.

Rnd 5: (2 Sc in next sc, sc in next 3 sc) around:
30 sc.

Rnd 6: Sc in Back Loop Only of each sc around
(*Fig. 1, page 42*).

Rnds 7-33: Sc in both loops of each sc around.

Rnd 34: Working in Back Loops Only, (decrease,
sc in next 3 sc) around changing to Brown in last sc
made: 24 sc.

Rnd 35: (Decrease, sc in next 2 sc) around: 18 sc.

Stuff Log firmly with fiberfill.

Rnd 36: (Decrease, sc in next sc) around: 12 sc.

Rnd 37: Decrease around; slip st in next sc,
finish off leaving a long end for sewing: 6 sc.

Thread needle with long end, weave needle
through sc on Rnd 37; gather **tightly** to close and
secure end.

TWIG
Rnd 1 (Right side): With Dk Brown, ch 2; 6 sc in
second ch from hook; do **not** join, place marker to
mark beginning of rnd.

Rnds 2 and 3: Sc in each sc around.

Rnd 4: Sc in each sc around; finish off leaving a
long end for sewing.

Stuff Twig lightly with fiberfill.

BRANCH

Rnd 1 (Right side): With Dk Brown, ch 2; 8 sc in second ch from hook; do **not** join, place marker to mark beginning of rnd.

Rnds 2-7: Sc in each sc around.

Rnd 8: Sc in each around; finish off leaving a long end for sewing.

Stuff Branch lightly with fiberfill.

LEAF (Make 2)
With Dk Green, ch 5.

Rnd 1 (Right side): 2 Dc in third ch from hook, 2 hdc in next ch, 4 sc in last ch; working in free loops of beginning ch **(Fig. 3, page 42)**, 2 hdc in next ch, 2 dc in same ch as first dc; join with slip st to top of beginning ch, finish off leaving a long end for sewing: 13 sts.

Using photo as a guide:
Sew one Leaf to end of Twig and Branch.
Sew Twig to side of Branch.
Sew Branch to Log.

FRANNIE
BODY

Rnd 1 (Right side): With Green, ch 2; 6 sc in second ch from hook; do **not** join, place marker to mark beginning of rnd **(see Markers, page 42)**.

Rnd 2: 2 Sc in each sc around: 12 sc.

Rnd 3: (2 Sc in next sc, sc in next sc) around: 18 sc.

Rnd 4: (2 Sc in next sc, sc in next 2 sc) around: 24 sc.

Rnd 5: (2 Sc in next sc, sc in next 3 sc) around: 30 sc.

Rnds 6-15: Sc in each sc around.

Slip loop from hook onto safety pin to prevent work from unraveling while attaching eyes. Using photo as a guide, attach eyes to Body on Rnd 8.

Rnd 16: Slip loop from safety pin onto hook; (decrease, sc in next 3 sc) around: 24 sc.

Rnd 17: (Decrease, sc in next 2 sc) around: 18 sc.

Stuff Body firmly with fiberfill.

Rnd 18: (Decrease, sc in next sc) around: 12 sc.

Rnd 19: Decrease around; slip st in next sc, finish off leaving a long end for sewing: 6 sc.

Thread needle with long end, weave needle through sc on Rnd 19; gather **tightly** to close and secure end.

Instructions continued on page 22.

WING (Make 2)

Rnd 1 (Right side): With Green, ch 2; 6 sc in second ch from hook; do **not** join, place marker to mark beginning of rnd.

Rnd 2: 2 Sc in each sc around: 12 sc.

Rnds 3 and 4: Sc in each around.

Rnd 5: (Decrease, sc in next sc) around; slip st in next sc, finish off leaving a long end for sewing: 8 sc.

Beginning at slip st, flatten Rnd 5. Using photo as a guide and working through all thicknesses, sew Wings to Body on Rnds 9-11.

BEAK

Rnd 1 (Right side): With Dk Brown, ch 2; 8 sc in second ch from hook; do **not** join, place marker to mark beginning of rnd.

Rnd 2: 2 Sc in each sc around: 16 sc.

Rnd 3: (2 Sc in next sc, sc in next sc) around; slip st in next sc: 24 sc.

Joining Row: Beginning at slip st, fold Beak with **wrong** side together and matching sts on Rnd 3. Ch 1, working through **both** thicknesses, sc in each sc across stuffing Beak lightly with fiberfill before closing; finish off leaving a long end for sewing.

Using photo as a guide, page 21:
Sew Beak to Body between eyes.
Sew Bird to Log.

SMALL BIRD

Make one Bird using Blue for Body and Wings, and Brown for Beak.
Make one Bird using Brown for Body and Wings, and Dk Brown for Beak.

BODY

Rnd 1 (Right side): Ch 2, 6 sc in second ch from hook; do **not** join, place marker to mark beginning of rnd *(see Markers, page 42)*.

Rnd 2: 2 Sc in each sc around: 12 sc.

Rnd 3: (2 Sc in next sc, sc in next sc) around: 18 sc.

Rnds 4-10: Sc in each sc around.

Slip loop from hook onto safety pin to prevent work from unraveling while attaching eyes. Using photo as a guide, page 23, attach eyes to Body on Rnd 5.

Rnd 11: Slip loop from safety pin onto hook; (decrease, sc in next sc) around: 12 sc.

Stuff Body firmly with fiberfill.

Rnd 12: Decrease around; slip st in next sc, finish off leaving a long end for sewing: 6 sc.

Thread needle with long end, weave needle through sc on Rnd 12; gather **tightly** to close and secure end.

WING (Make 2)

Rnd 1 (Right side): Ch 2, 5 sc in second ch from hook; do **not** join, place marker to mark beginning of rnd.

Rnd 2: 2 Sc in each sc around: 10 sc.

Rnd 3: Sc in each sc around.

Rnd 4: Decrease around; slip st in next sc, finish off leaving a long end for sewing: 5 sc.

Beginning at slip st, flatten Rnd 4. Using photo as a guide and working through all thicknesses, sew Wings to Body on Rnds 5-7.

BEAK

Rnd 1 (Right side): Ch 2, 8 sc in second ch from hook; do **not** join, place marker to mark beginning of rnd.

Rnd 2: 2 Sc in each sc around; slip st in next sc: 16 sc.

Joining Row: Beginning at slip st, fold Beak with **wrong** side together and matching sts on Rnd 2. Ch 1, working through **both** thicknesses, sc in each sc across; finish off leaving a long end for sewing.

Using photo as a guide:
Sew Brown Beak to Blue Body between eyes.
Sew Dk Brown Beak to Brown Body between eyes.

Wrap heavy duty thread around plastic ring and secure. Leaving a 3" (7.5 cm) length, attach thread to top of Large Bird.

Using heavy duty thread, attach thread to bottom left edge of Log and leaving a 3½" (9 cm) length, attach thread to top of Small Blue Bird. Using heavy duty thread, attach thread to bottom right edge of Log and leaving a 5" (12.5 cm) length, attach thread to top of Small Brown Bird.

slowBOAT &
TRAPEZE

Slowboat and tiny Trapeze live in a patch of daisies beside Thoreau's mushroom barn. Slowboat was Thoreau's head gardener until the elderly snail got too sluggish to do the job. Now he's quietly retired with a nice pension. However, there's nothing quiet about young Trapeze. The tyke spends his days zipping around (at an inch per minute), asking Slowboat endless questions about anything and everything. Early one recent morning, the young snail decided to inch over to the mushroom barn so he could visit Thoreau. When he got there, the barn door was closed. Undaunted, the youngster began climbing the door to see how far up he could go. He got a good way off the ground before Farmer Jones bolted out of the barn, late for market with a heap of mushroom baskets. With the sudden *bang!* of the door, Trapeze lost his grip and went sailing through the air—all the way back to the daisy patch! Fortunately, he landed on a cushy gerbera. It's kind of a good thing for Slowboat that the old snail's gotten a bit hard of hearing, because all Trapeze talks about now is the day he learned how to fly.

Finished Sizes
Slowboat - 4" (10 cm) tall
Trapeze - 2³/₄" (7 cm) tall
Mushroom - 2¹/₂" (6.5 cm) tall

MATERIALS

Medium Weight Yarn
[6 ounces, 312 yards
(170 grams, 285 meters) per skein]:
Blue, Green, Red, Gold, Brown, **and** White
- 1 skein **each** color
Crochet hook, size G (4 mm) **or** size needed
for gauge
6 mm Doll eyes - 4
Polyester fiberfill
Stuffing pellets
Yarn needle
Safety pin

GAUGE: 16 sc and 18 rows/rnds = 4" (10 cm)

Gauge Swatch: 4" (10 cm) square
Ch 17.
Row 1: Sc in second ch from hook and in each ch
across: 16 sc.
Rows 2-18: Ch 1, turn; sc in each sc across.
Finish off.

STITCH GUIDE
● **DECREASE**
● Pull up a loop in next 2 sc, YO and draw
● through all 3 loops on hook (**counts as one sc**).

SLOWBOAT
HEAD & BODY

Rnd 1 (Right side)**:** With Blue, ch 2; 6 sc in second ch from hook; do **not** join, place marker to mark beginning of rnd (**see Markers, page 42**).

Rnd 2: 2 Sc in each sc around: 12 sc.

Rnd 3: (2 Sc in next sc, sc in next sc) around: 18 sc.

Rnds 4-8: Sc in each sc around.

Slip loop from hook onto safety pin to prevent work from unraveling while attaching eyes. Using photo as a guide, page 27, attach eyes to Head & Body on Rnd 5.

Rnd 9: Slip loop from safety pin onto hook; sc in each sc around.

Rnds 10-13: Sc in each sc around.

Rnd 14: (Decrease, sc in next 7 sc) twice: 16 sc.

Rnd 15: Sc in each sc around.

Rnd 16: (Decrease, sc in next 6 sc) twice: 14 sc.

Rnd 17: Sc in each sc around.

Rnd 18: (Decrease, sc in next 5 sc) twice: 12 sc.

Rnd 19: Sc in each sc around.

Stuff Head & Body with fiberfill.

Rnd 20: (Decrease, sc in next 4 sc) twice: 10 sc.

Rnd 21: Sc in each sc around.

Rnd 22: (Decrease, sc in next 3 sc) twice: 8 sc.

Rnd 23: Sc in each sc around.

Rnd 24: (Decrease, sc in next 2 sc) twice: 6 sc.

Rnd 25: Sc in each sc around.

Rnd 26: (Decrease, sc in next sc) twice: 4 sc.

Rnd 27: Sc in each sc around.

Rnd 28: Decrease twice; slip st in next sc, finish off leaving a long end for sewing: 2 sc.

Thread needle with long end, weave needle through sc on Rnd 28; gather **tightly** to close and secure end.

SHELL

Rnd 1 (Right side): With Green, ch 2; 6 sc in second ch from hook; do **not** join, place marker to mark beginning of rnd.

Rnd 2: 2 Sc in Back Loop Only of each sc around (*Fig. 1, page 42*): 12 sc.

Rnd 3: Working in Back Loops Only, (2 sc in next sc, sc in next sc) around: 18 sc.

Rnd 4: Working in Back Loops Only, (2 sc in next sc, sc in next 2 sc) around: 24 sc.

Rnd 5: Working in Back Loops Only, (2 sc in next sc, sc in next 3 sc) around: 30 sc.

Rnds 6-8: Working in both loops, sc in each sc around.

Rnd 9: Working in Back Loops Only, (decrease, sc in next 3 sc) around: 24 sc.

Rnd 10: Working in Back Loops Only, (decrease, sc in next 2 sc) around: 18 sc.

Rnd 11: Working in Back Loops Only, (decrease, sc in next sc) around: 12 sc.

Stuff Shell with fiberfill.

Rnd 12: Working in Back Loops Only, decrease around; slip st in next sc, finish off leaving a long end for sewing: 6 sc.

Thread needle with long end, weave needle through sc on Rnd 12; gather **tightly** to close and secure end.

Using photo as a guide, sew Shell to Body.

ANTENNAE

Tie a knot in the end of a 6" (15 cm) length of Blue. Trim yarn close to knot. Thread needle with free end and attach yarn to Rnd 2 at side of top on Head, 1/2" (12 mm) below knot. Insert needle into Head and come out on opposite side of top on Head; secure yarn. Tie a knot 1/2" (12 mm) from Head. Trim yarn close to knot.

Using backstitch (*Fig. 4, page 43*) and Red, add mouth.

Instructions continued on page 28.

TRAPEZE
HEAD & BODY

Rnd 1 (Right side): With Gold, ch 2; 6 sc in second ch from hook; do **not** join, place marker to mark beginning of rnd (*see Markers, page 42*).

Rnd 2: 2 Sc in each sc around: 12 sc.

Rnds 3-7: Sc in each sc around.

Slip loop from hook onto safety pin to prevent work from unraveling while attaching eyes. Using photo as a guide, page 29, attach eyes to Head & Body on Rnd 4.

Rnd 8: Slip loop from safety pin to hook; sc in each sc around.

Rnds 9-12: Sc in each sc around.

Rnd 13: (Decrease, sc in next 4 sc) twice: 10 sc.

Rnd 14: Sc in each sc around.

Rnd 15: (Decrease, sc in next 3 sc) twice: 8 sc.

Rnd 16: Sc in each sc around.

Stuff Head & Body lightly with fiberfill.

Rnd 17: (Decrease, sc in next 2 sc) twice: 6 sc.

Rnd 18: Sc in each sc around.

Rnd 19: (Decrease, sc in next sc) twice: 4 sc.

Rnd 20: Sc in each sc around.

Rnd 21: Decrease twice; slip st in next sc, finish off leaving a long end for sewing: 2 sc.

Thread needle with long end, weave needle through sc on Rnd 21; gather **tightly** to close and secure end.

SHELL

Rnd 1 (Right side): With Brown, ch 2; 6 sc in second ch from hook; do **not** join, place marker to mark beginning of rnd.

Rnd 2: 2 Sc in Back Loop Only of each sc around (*Fig. 1, page 42*): 12 sc.

Rnd 3: Working in Back Loops Only, (2 sc in next sc, sc in next sc) around: 18 sc.

Rnds 4 and 5: Working in both loops, sc in each sc around.

Rnd 6: Working in Back Loops Only, (decrease, sc in next sc) around: 12 sc.

Stuff Shell firmly with fiberfill.

Rnd 7: Working in Back Loops Only, decrease around; slip st in next sc, finish off leaving a long end for sewing: 6 sc.

Thread needle with long end, weave needle through sc on Rnd 7; gather **tightly** to close and secure end.

Using photo as a guide, sew Shell to Body.

ANTENNAE

Tie a knot in the end of a 6" (15 cm) length of Gold. Trim yarn close to knot. Thread needle with free end and attach yarn to Rnd 2 at side of top on Head, 1/2" (12 mm) below knot. Insert needle into Head and come out on opposite side of top on Head; secure yarn. Tie a knot 1/2" (12 mm) from Head. Trim yarn close to knot.

Using straight stitch (*Fig. 6, page 43*) and Brown, add mouth.

MUSHROOM

Rnd 1 (Right side): With White, ch 2; 6 sc in second ch from hook; do **not** join, place marker to mark beginning of rnd (see Markers, page 42).

Rnd 2: 2 Sc in each sc around: 12 sc.

Rnd 3: (2 Sc in next sc, sc in next sc) around: 18 sc.

Rnd 4: Sc in Back Loop Only of each sc around (Fig. 1, page 42).

Rnds 5 and 6: Sc in both loops of each sc around.

Rnd 7: Sc in each sc around changing to Red in last sc made (Fig. 2, page 42).

Rnd 8: (2 Sc in next sc, sc in next 2 sc) around: 24 sc.

Rnd 9: (2 Sc in next sc, sc in next 3 sc) around: 30 sc.

Rnd 10: (2 Sc in next sc, sc in next 4 sc) around: 36 sc.

Rnd 11: Sc in Back Loop Only of each sc around.

Rnds 12-15: Sc in both loops of each sc around.

Rnd 16: (Decrease, sc in next 4 sc) around: 30 sc.

Rnd 17: (Decrease, sc in next 3 sc) around: 24 sc.

Rnd 18: (Decrease, sc in next 2 sc) around: 18 sc.

Rnd 19: (Decrease, sc in next sc) around: 12 sc.

Fill stem with pellets, then stuff remaining Mushroom firmly with fiberfill.

Rnd 20: Decrease around; slip st in next sc, finish off leaving a long end for sewing: 6 sc.

Thread needle with long end, weave needle through sc on Rnd 20; gather **tightly** to close and secure end.

LARGE SPOT

Rnd 1 (Right side): With White, ch 2; 6 sc in second ch from hook; do **not** join, place marker to mark beginning of rnd.

Rnd 2: 2 Sc in each sc around; slip st in next sc, finish off leaving a long end for sewing: 12 sc.

SMALL SPOT (Make 2)

Rnd 1 (Right side): With White, ch 2; 6 sc in second ch from hook; join with slip st to first sc, finish off leaving a long end for sewing.

Using photo as a guide:
Sew Spots to Mushroom.
Sew Small Snail to top of Mushroom.

westinghouse

Westinghouse and his Pine Forest buddies used to travel really fast on overhead power lines! You see, the squirrel gang didn't rely on the paw-over-paw method. Westie's bunch found an old red skateboard in a ditch. Sure, it was rusty, with wheels that squeaked terribly. But once it was hauled atop a telephone pole and balanced on two wires, it could go like greased lightning! Westinghouse, Edison, and Tesla became infamous for their rowdy raids on the Oak Woods. They would fly along the wires on the squeaking skateboard. Down, down from Pine Forest, faster and faster they'd go, until they reached the other side of the valley. At the Oak Woods, they'd hit the ground running, grabbing all the mushrooms and acorns they could carry before scampering back to the skateboard. They'd zip back home, singing in time to the *squeak-squeak* of the wheels. This grand adventure lasted all through the autumn months until a county lineman retrieved the skateboard from the top of a pole, shaking his head and muttering, "Dang kids." Old Westie still spins tales about his days as a Skateboard Squirrel. Some are true. Some are not. But all are fun to hear.

Finished Size: 6" (15 cm) tall

MATERIALS

Medium Weight Yarn [**MEDIUM 4**]
  [3.5 ounces, 170 yards
  (100 grams, 156 meters) per skein]:
    Lt Brown, Green, Brown, Tan, and Dk Brown
    - 1 skein **each** color
  [6 ounces, 312 yards
  (170 grams, 285 meters) per skein]:
    Red - small amount   [**BULKY 5**]
Bulky Weight Novelty Yarn
  [1.75 ounces, 64 yards
  (50 grams, 58 meters) per skein]:
    Copper - 1 skein
Crochet hook, size G (4 mm) **or** size needed
  for gauge
6 mm Doll eyes - 2
Polyester fiberfill
Yarn needle
Safety pin

GAUGE: 16 sc and 18 rows/rnds = 4" (10 cm)

Gauge Swatch: 4" (10 cm) square
Ch 17.
Row 1: Sc in second ch from hook and in each ch across: 16 sc.
Rows 2-18: Ch 1, turn; sc in each sc across.
Finish off.

STITCH GUIDE
● **DECREASE**
● Pull up a loop in next 2 sc, YO and draw
● through all 3 loops on hook (**counts as one sc**).

WESTINGHOUSE
HEAD

Rnd 1 (Right side): With Lt Brown, ch 2; 6 sc in second ch from hook; do **not** join, place marker to mark beginning of rnd *(see Markers, page 42)*.

Rnd 2: 2 Sc in each sc around: 12 sc.

Rnd 3: (2 Sc in next sc, sc in next sc) around: 18 sc.

Rnd 4: (2 Sc in next sc, sc in next 2 sc) around: 24 sc.

Rnds 5-7: Sc in each sc around.

Rnd 8: 2 Sc in each of next 4 sc (cheek), sc in next 2 sc, 2 sc in each of next 2 sc (nose), sc in next 2 sc, 2 sc in each of next 4 sc (cheek), sc in next 10 sc: 34 sc.

Rnds 9 and 10: Sc in each sc around.

Slip loop from hook onto safety pin to prevent work from unraveling while attaching eyes. Using photo as a guide, attach eyes to Head on Rnd 8.

Rnd 11: Slip loop from safety pin onto hook; decrease 4 times, sc in next 2 sc, decrease twice, sc in next 2 sc, decrease 4 times, sc in next 10 sc: 24 sc.

Rnd 12: Sc in each sc around.

Rnd 13: (Decrease, sc in next 2 sc) around: 18 sc.

Rnd 14 (neck): Sc in each sc around.

Stuff Head firmly with fiberfill.

BODY

Rnd 1: (2 Sc in next sc, sc in next 2 sc) around: 24 sc.

Rnd 2: (2 Sc in next sc, sc in next 3 sc) around: 30 sc.

Rnd 3: (2 Sc in next sc, sc in next 4 sc) around: 36 sc.

Rnds 4-13: Sc in each sc around.

Rnd 14: (Decrease, sc in next 4 sc) around: 30 sc.

Rnd 15: (Decrease, sc in next 3 sc) around: 24 sc.

Rnd 16: (Decrease, sc in next 2 sc) around: 18 sc.

Stuff Body firmly with fiberfill.

Rnd 17: (Decrease, sc in next sc) around: 12 sc.

Rnd 18: Decrease around; slip st in next sc, finish off leaving a long end for sewing: 6 sc.

Thread needle with long end, weave needle through sc on Rnd 18; gather **tightly** to close and secure end.

EAR (Make 2)

Rnd 1 (Right side): With Lt Brown, ch 2; 4 sc in second ch from hook; do **not** join, place marker to mark beginning of rnd.

Rnd 2: (2 Sc in next sc, sc in next sc) twice: 6 sc.

Rnd 3: Sc in each sc around; slip st in next sc, finish off leaving a long end for sewing.

Beginning at slip st, fold Ear with **wrong** side together and matching sts on Rnd 3. Ch 1, working through **both** thicknesses, sc in each sc across; finish off leaving a long end for sewing. Using photo as a guide and working through both thicknesses, sew Ears to Rnds 2-4 on Head.

ARM (Make 2)

Rnd 1 (Right side): With Lt Brown, ch 2; 8 sc in second ch from hook; do **not** join, place marker to mark beginning of rnd.

Rnds 2-6: Sc in each sc around.

Rnd 7: (Decrease, sc in next 2 sc) twice; slip st in next sc, finish off leaving a long end for sewing: 6 sc.

Stuff bottom of Arm lightly with fiberfill. Beginning at slip st, flatten Rnd 7. Using photo as a guide and working through all thicknesses, sew Arms to Body on Rnd 1.

FOOT (Make 2)

Rnd 1 (Right side): With Lt Brown, ch 2; 8 sc in second ch from hook; do **not** join, place marker to mark beginning of rnd.

Rnds 2 and 3: Sc in each sc around.

Rnd 4: Sc in each sc around; slip st in next sc, finish off leaving a long end for sewing.

Stuff bottom of Foot lightly with fiberfill. Beginning at slip st, flatten Rnd 4. Using photo as a guide and working through all thicknesses, sew Feet to bottom front of Body.

TAIL

Rnd 1 (Right side): Holding two strands of Copper together, ch 2; 4 sc in second ch from hook; do **not** join, place marker to mark beginning of rnd.

Rnd 2: 2 Sc in each sc around: 8 sc.

Rnd 3: (2 Sc in next sc, sc in next sc) around: 12 sc.

Rnd 4: (2 Sc in next sc, sc in next 2 sc) around: 16 sc.

Rnd 5: (2 Sc in next sc, sc in next 3 sc) around: 20 sc.

Instructions continued on page 34.

Rnd 6: (2 Sc in next sc, sc in next 4 sc) around: 24 sc.

Rnds 7-25: Sc in each sc around.

Rnd 26: (Decrease, sc in next 2 sc) around; slip st in next sc, finish off leaving a long end for sewing: 18 sc.

Beginning at slip st, flatten Rnd 26. Using photo as a guide and working through all thicknesses, sew Tail to Body on Rnd 23.

Using Lt Brown, tack Tail to back of neck on Body.

Using photo as a guide, satin stitch *(Fig. 5, page 43)* and straight stitch *(Fig. 6, page 43)*, add Brown nose to Head.

ACORN
NUT

Rnd 1 (Right side)**:** With Brown, ch 2; 4 sc in second ch from hook; do **not** join, place marker to mark beginning of rnd *(see Markers, page 42)*.

Rnd 2: (2 Sc in next sc, sc in next sc) twice: 6 sc.

Rnd 3: (2 Sc in next sc, sc in next 2 sc) around: 8 sc.

Rnd 4: (2 Sc in next sc, sc in next 3 sc) around: 10 sc.

Rnd 5: (2 Sc in next sc, sc in next 4 sc) around: 12 sc.

Rnds 6-8: Sc in each sc around.

Stuff Nut firmly with fiberfill.

Rnd 9: Decrease around; slip st in next sc, finish off leaving a long end for sewing: 6 sc.

Thread needle with long end, weave needle through sc on Rnd 9; gather **tightly** to close and secure end.

CAP

Rnd 1 (Right side)**:** With Dk Brown and leaving a long end for making loop, ch 2; 12 sc in second ch from hook; do **not** join, place marker to mark beginning of rnd.

Rnd 2: 2 Sc in each sc around: 24 sc.

Rnds 3 and 4: Sc in each sc around.

Rnd 5: Decrease around; slip st in next sc, finish off: 12 sc.

Using long end, make a ¹/₂" (12 mm) loop on top of Cap, secure end.
Using photo as a guide, slide Cap onto Nut.

MUSHROOM

Rnd 1 (Right side)**:** With Tan, ch 2; 6 sc in second ch from hook; do **not** join, place marker to mark beginning of rnd *(see Markers, page 42)*.

Rnd 2: 2 Sc in each sc around: 12 sc.

Rnd 3: Sc in Back Loop Only of each sc around *(Fig. 1, page 42)*.

Rnds 4-7: Sc in both loops of each sc around.

Rnd 8: Sc in each sc around changing to Brown in last sc made.

Rnd 9: (2 Sc in next sc, sc in next sc) around: 18 sc.

Rnd 10: (2 Sc in next sc, sc in next 2 sc) around: 24 sc.

Rnd 11: Sc in Back Loop Only of each sc around.

Rnds 12-15: Sc in both loops of each sc around.

Rnd 16: (Decrease, sc in next 2 sc) around: 18 sc.

Stuff Mushroom firmly with fiberfill.

Rnd 17: (Decrease, sc in next sc) around: 12 sc.

Rnd 18: Decrease around; slip st in next sc, finish off leaving a long end for sewing: 6 sc.

Thread needle with long end, weave needle through sc on Rnd 18; gather **tightly** to close and secure end.

LARGE SPOT
Rnd 1 (Right side): With Tan, ch 2; 6 sc in second ch from hook; do **not** join, place marker to mark beginning of rnd.

Rnd 2: 2 Sc in each sc around; slip st in next sc, finish off leaving a long end for sewing: 12 sc.

SMALL SPOT (Make 2)
Rnd 1 (Right side): With Tan, ch 2; 6 sc in second ch from hook; join with slip st to first sc, finish off leaving a long end for sewing.

Using photo as a guide, page 30, sew Spots to Mushroom.

FLOWER
Rnd 1 (Right side): With Red, ch 2; 5 sc in second ch from hook; do **not** join, place marker to mark beginning of rnd.

Rnd 2: (2 Dc, slip st) in each sc around; slip st in next dc, finish off leaving a long end for sewing.

Using Tan and straight stitch (**Fig. 6, page 43**), work an "X" in center of Flower, attaching it to the base of the Mushroom.

LAWN
Rnd 1 (Right side): With Green, ch 2; 6 sc in second ch from hook; do **not** join, place marker to mark beginning of rnd (see Markers, page 42).

Rnd 2: 2 Sc in each sc around: 12 sc.

Rnd 3: (2 Sc in next sc, sc in next sc) around: 18 sc.

Rnd 4: (2 Sc in next sc, sc in next 2 sc) around: 24 sc.

Rnd 5: (2 Sc in next sc, sc in next 3 sc) around: 30 sc.

Rnd 6: (2 Sc in next sc, sc in next 4 sc) around: 36 sc.

Rnd 7: (2 Sc in next sc, sc in next 5 sc) around: 42 sc.

Rnd 8: (2 Sc in next sc, sc in next 6 sc) around: 48 sc.

Rnd 9: (2 Sc in next sc, sc in next 7 sc) around: 54 sc.

Rnd 10: (2 Sc in next sc, sc in next 8 sc) around: 60 sc.

Rnd 11: (2 Sc in next sc, sc in next 9 sc) around: 66 sc.

Rnd 12: (2 Sc in next sc, sc in next 10 sc) around: 72 sc.

Rnd 13: (2 Sc in next sc, sc in next 11 sc) around: 78 sc.

Rnd 14: (2 Sc in next sc, sc in next 12 sc) around; slip st in next sc, finish off: 84 sc.

All pieces may be left separate or sewn to the Lawn.

shalimar

What do you think—does Shalimar's white stripe make her look old? The sweet-natured skunk recently had a birthday and believes she's arrived at her middle years. She's still slim and trim, but she thinks the stripe that used to be rather dashing is now a bit aging. She's seriously considering a visit to Beatrix. After all, hair color is a popular way to keep oneself fresh—one's appearance, that is. But if she colors her stripe, will everyone laugh? It's not as though blonde, brunette, or redhaired skunks are an everyday sight. She could dye the white hair black, but that seems just a tad over-the-top. A trip to the Hoot, Hoot, Whooray! Café may be helpful. Hedda always has the right words to make Shalimar feel better. While she's there, a free-range chicken sandwich with poppyseed yogurt dressing (mango-tofu cheesecake on the side) will surely put everything into perspective.

Finished Size: 5³/₄" (14.5 cm) tall

MATERIALS
Medium Weight Yarn [MEDIUM 4]
  [3.5 ounces, 195 yards
  (100 grams, 175 meters) per skein]:
    Black - 1 skein [BULKY 5]
Bulky Weight Yarn
  [3.5 ounces, 180 yards
  (100 grams, 165 meters) per skein]:
    White - skein
Crochet hook, size G (4 mm) **or** size needed
  for gauge
9 mm Doll eyes - 2
Polyester fiberfill
Felt - small piece of white for eye patches
Embroidery floss - small amount of pink
  and white
Sewing needle
Yarn needle
Safety pin

GAUGE: 16 sc and 18 rows/rnds = 4" (10 cm)

Gauge Swatch: 4" (10 cm) square
Ch 17.
Row 1: Sc in second ch from hook and in each ch
across: 16 sc.
Rows 2-18: Ch 1, turn; sc in each sc across.
Finish off.

STITCH GUIDE
● **DECREASE**
● Pull up a loop in next 2 sc, YO and draw
● through all 3 loops on hook (**counts as one sc**).

SHALIMAR
HEAD

Rnd 1 (Right side)**:** With Black, ch 2; 6 sc in second
ch from hook; do **not** join, place marker to mark
beginning of rnd (*see Markers, page 42*).

Rnd 2: 2 Sc in each sc around: 12 sc.

Rnd 3: (2 Sc in next sc, sc in next sc) around: 18 sc.

Rnd 4: (2 Sc in next sc, sc in next 2 sc) around:
24 sc.

Rnds 5-7: Sc in each sc around.

Rnd 8: Sc in next 11 sc, 2 sc in each of next 2 sc
(nose), sc in next 11 sc: 26 sc.

Rnd 9: Sc in next 12 sc, 2 sc in each of next 2 sc,
sc in next 12 sc: 28 sc.

Rnd 10: Sc in next 10 sc, decrease 4 times, sc in
next 10 sc: 24 sc.

Slip loop from hook onto safety pin to prevent
work from unraveling while attaching eyes.
Cut two Eye Patches from White felt.

EYE PATCH PATTERN

Using photo as a guide, insert an eye through
each Eye Patch and attach to Head on Rnd 7.

Rnd 11: Slip loop from safety pin onto hook;
(decrease, 2 sc in next sc) around: 18 sc.

Rnd 12: (Decrease, sc in next sc) around: 12 sc.

Stuff Head firmly with fiberfill.

Rnd 13 (neck)**:** (2 Sc in next sc, sc in next sc)
around: 18 sc.

BODY

Rnds 1-11: Sc in each sc around.

Rnd 12: (Decrease, sc in next sc) around: 12 sc.

Stuff Body firmly with fiberfill.

Rnd 13: Decrease around; slip st in next sc, finish off leaving a long end for sewing: 6 sc.

Thread needle with long end, weave needle through sc on Rnd 13; gather **tightly** to close and secure end.

HEAD STRIPE

Row 1 (Right side)**:** With White, ch 2; 2 sc in second ch from hook: 2 sc.

 Note Loop a short piece of yarn around any stitch to mark Row 1 as **right** side.

Row 2: Ch 1, turn; 2 sc in first sc, sc in next sc: 3 sc.

Rows 3-5: Ch 1, turn; 2 sc in first sc, sc in each sc across: 6 sc.

Rows 6-11: Ch 1, turn; sc in each sc across.

Rows 12-15: Ch 1, turn; insert hook in first sc and in next sc, YO and draw through all 3 loops on hook (**counts as one sc**), sc in each sc across: 2 sc.

Row 16: Ch 1, turn; insert hook in first sc and in last sc, YO and draw through all 3 loops on hook (**counts as one sc**); finish off leaving a long end for sewing: one sc.

Using photo as a guide, page 40:
Sew Head Stripe to Head.
With pink floss and satin stitch (*Fig. 5, page 43*), embroider nose.

TAIL

Rnd 1 (Right side)**:** With Black, ch 2; 4 sc in second ch from hook; do **not** join, place marker to mark beginning of rnd.

Rnd 2: (2 Sc in next sc, sc in next sc) twice: 6 sc.

Rnd 3: (2 Sc in next sc, sc in next 2 sc) twice: 8 sc.

Rnd 4: (2 Sc in next sc, sc in next 3 sc) twice: 10 sc.

Rnd 5: (2 Sc in next sc, sc in next 4 sc) twice: 12 sc.

Rnd 6: (2 Sc in next sc, sc in next 5 sc) twice: 14 sc.

Rnd 7: (2 Sc in next sc, sc in next 6 sc) twice: 16 sc.

Rnd 8: (2 Sc in next sc, sc in next 7 sc) twice: 18 sc.

Rnd 9: (2 Sc in next sc, sc in next 8 sc) twice: 20 sc.

Rnd 10: (2 Sc in next sc, sc in next 9 sc) twice: 22 sc.

Rnd 11: (2 Sc in next sc, sc in next 10 sc) twice: 24 sc.

Rnds 12-20: Sc in each sc around.

Rnd 21: (Decrease, sc in next 10 sc) twice: 22 sc.

Rnd 22: (Decrease, sc in next 9 sc) twice: 20 sc.

Rnd 23: (Decrease, sc in next 8 sc) twice: 18 sc.

Rnd 24: (Decrease, sc in next 7 sc) twice: 16 sc.

Rnd 25: (Decrease, sc in next 6 sc) twice: 14 sc.

Rnd 26: (Decrease, sc in next 5 sc) twice: 12 sc.

Stuff Tail lightly with fiberfill.

Rnd 27: Decrease around; slip st in next sc, finish off leaving a long end for sewing: 6 sc.

Thread needle with long end, weave needle through sc on Rnd 27; gather **tightly** to close and secure end.

Instructions continued on page 40.

TAIL STRIPE

Row 1 (Right side)**:** With White, ch 2; 2 sc in second ch from hook: 2 sc.

 Note Mark Row 1 as **right** side.

Row 2: Ch 1, turn; 2 sc in first sc, sc in next sc: 3 sc.

Rows 3-5: Ch 1, turn; 2 sc in first sc, sc in each sc across: 6 sc.

Row 6: Ch 1, turn; sc in each sc across.

Repeat Row 6 until piece measures same length as Tail; finish off leaving a long end for sewing.

Sew Tail Stripe to Tail.

Using photo as a guide, sew Tail to Body on Rnd 11. Tack back of the Tail to back of Body at neck.

LEG (Make 4)

Rnd 1 (Right side)**:** With Black, ch 2; 8 sc in second ch from hook; do **not** join, place marker to mark beginning of rnd.

Rnds 2-4: Sc in each sc around.

Rnd 5: Sc in each sc around; slip st in next sc, finish off leaving a long end for sewing.

Stuff bottom of Legs lightly with fiberfill. Beginning at slip st, flatten Rnd 5. Using photo as a guide and working through all thicknesses, sew two Legs to upper Body at neck and two Legs to bottom of Body.

EAR (Make 2)

Rnd 1 (Right side)**:** With Black, ch 2; 4 sc in second ch from hook; do **not** join, place marker to mark beginning of rnd.

Rnd 2: Sc in each sc around.

Rnd 3: Sc in each sc around; slip st in next sc, finish off leaving a long end for sewing.

Beginning at slip st, flatten Rnd 3. Using photo as a guide and working through all thicknesses, sew Ears to Head.

general INSTRUCTIONS

ABBREVIATIONS

ch(s)	chain(s)
cm	centimeters
dc	double crochet(s)
hdc	half double crochet(s)
mm	millimeters
Rnd(s)	Round(s)
sc	single crochet(s)
st(s)	stitch(es)
YO	yarn over

( ) or [ ] — work enclosed instructions **as many** times as specified by the number immediately following **or** work all enclosed instructions in the stitch or space indicated **or** contains explanatory remarks.

colon (:) — the number(s) given after a colon at the end of a row or round denote(s) the number of stitches you should have on that row or round.

CROCHET TERMINOLOGY

UNITED STATES		INTERNATIONAL
slip stitch (slip st)	=	single crochet (sc)
single crochet (sc)	=	double crochet (dc)
half double crochet (hdc)	=	half treble crochet (htr)
double crochet (dc)	=	treble crochet (tr)
treble crochet (tr)	=	double treble crochet (dtr)
double treble crochet (dtr)	=	triple treble crochet (ttr)
triple treble crochet (tr tr)	=	quadruple treble crochet (qtr)
skip	=	miss

Yarn Weight Symbol & Names	LACE 0	SUPER FINE 1	FINE 2	LIGHT 3	MEDIUM 4	BULKY 5	SUPER BULKY 6
Type of Yarns in Category	Fingering, 10-count crochet thread	Sock, Fingering Baby	Sport, Baby	DK, Light Worsted	Worsted, Afghan, Aran	Chunky, Craft, Rug	Bulky, Roving
Crochet Gauge* Ranges in Single Crochet to 4" (10 cm)	32-42 double crochets**	21-32 sts	16-20 sts	12-17 sts	11-14 sts	8-11 sts	5-9 sts
Advised Hook Size Range	Steel*** 6,7,8 Regular hook B-1	B-1 to E-4	E-4 to 7	7 to I-9	I-9 to K-10.5	K-10.5 to M-13	M-13 and larger

*GUIDELINES ONLY: The chart above reflects the most commonly used gauges and hook sizes for specific yarn categories.

** Lace weight yarns are usually crocheted on larger-size hooks to create lacy openwork patterns. Accordingly, a gauge range is difficult to determine. Always follow the gauge stated in your pattern.

*** Steel crochet hooks are sized differently from regular hooks–the higher the number the smaller the hook, which is the reverse of regular hook sizing.

CROCHET HOOKS

U.S.	B-1	C-2	D-3	E-4	F-5	G-6	H-8	I-9	J-10	K-10½	N	P	Q
Metric - mm	2.25	2.75	3.25	3.5	3.75	4	5	5.5	6	6.5	9	10	15

◖■□□□ **BEGINNER**	Projects for first-time crocheters using basic stitches. Minimal shaping.
◖■■□□ **EASY**	Projects using yarn with basic stitches, repetitive stitch patterns, simple color changes, and simple shaping and finishing.
◖■■■□ **INTERMEDIATE**	Projects using a variety of techniques, such as basic lace patterns or color patterns, mid-level shaping and finishing.
◖■■■■ **EXPERIENCED**	Projects with intricate stitch patterns, techniques and dimension, such as non-repeating patterns, multi-color techniques, fine threads, small hooks, detailed shaping and refined finishing.

GAUGE

Exact gauge is **essential** for proper size. Before beginning your project, make the sample swatch given in the individual instructions in the yarn and hook specified. After completing the swatch, measure it, counting your stitches and rows carefully. If your swatch is larger or smaller than specified, **make another, changing hook size to get the correct gauge.** Keep trying until you find the size hook that will give you the specified gauge.

MARKERS

Markers are used to help distinguish the beginning of each round being worked. Place a 2" (5 cm) scrap piece of yarn before the first stitch of each round, moving marker after each round is complete.

BACK LOOP ONLY

Work only in loop(s) indicated by arrow **(Fig. 1)**.

Fig. 1

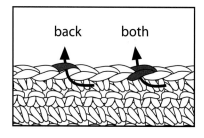

CHANGING COLORS

Insert hook in stitch indicated, YO and pull up a loop, cut yarn; with new yarn, YO and draw through both loops on hook **(Fig. 2)**.

Fig. 2

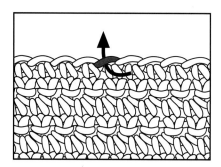

FREE LOOPS OF A CHAIN

When instructed to work in free loops of a chain, work in loop indicated by arrow **(Fig. 3)**.

Fig. 3

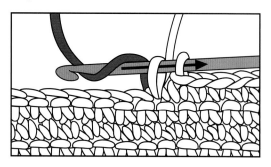

EMBROIDERY STITCHES
BACKSTITCH

The backstitch is worked from **right** to **left**. Come up at 1, go down at 2 and come up at 3 *(Fig. 4)*. The second stitch is made by going down at 1 and coming up at 4.

Fig. 4

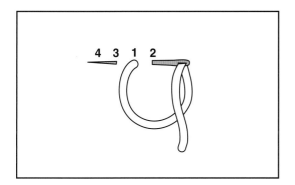

SATIN STITCH

Satin Stitch is a series of straight stitches worked side by side so they touch but do not overlap. Come up at odd number and go down at even number *(Fig. 5)*.

Fig. 5

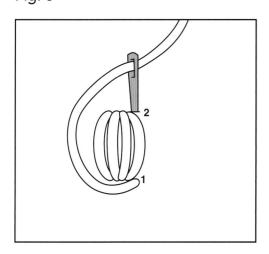

STRAIGHT STITCH

Straight Stitch is just what the name implies, a single, straight stitch. Come up at 1 and go down at 2 *(Fig. 6)*.

Fig. 6

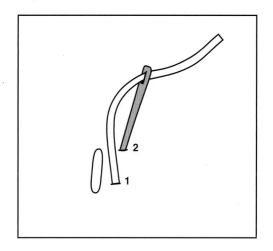

For digital downloads of Leisure Arts' best-selling designs, visit http://leisureartslibrary.com

Production Team: Instructional Editor - Lois J. Long; Technical Editor - Sarah J. Green; Editorial Writer - Susan McManus Johnson; Senior Graphic Artists - Lora Puls and Dana Vaughn; Photo Stylist - Sondra Daniel; and Photographer - Ken West.

yarn INFORMATION

Each item in this leaflet was made using various weights of yarn. Any brand of the specified weight of yarn may be used. It is best to refer to the yardage/meters when determining how many balls or skeins to purchase. Remember, to arrive at the finished size, it is the GAUGE/TENSION that is important, not the brand of yarn.

For your convenience, listed below are the specific yarns used to create our photography models.

THOREAU
Caron® Simply Soft®
Tan - #2604 Bone
Red Heart® Classic®
White - #1 White
Red - #914 Country Red
Black - #12 Black
Brown - #365 Coffee
Blue - #849 Olympic Blue
Green- #689 Forest Green
Yellow - #261 Maize

BEATRIX
Lion Brand® Vanna's Choice®
Ecru - #099 Linen
Brown - #126 Chocolate
Lion Brand® Fun Fur
Brown - #126 Chocolate

HEDDA & SYBLE
Lion Brand® Vanna's Choice®
White - #100 White
Dk Brown - #126 Chocolate
Brown - #124 Toffee
Lt Brown - #130 Honey

FRANNIE FINCH
Red Heart® Classic®
Dk Brown - #365 Coffee
Green - #622 Pale Sage
Brown - #339 Mid Brown
Blue - #882 Country Blue
Dk Green - #689 Forest Green

SLOWBOAT & TRAPEZE
TLC® Essentials™
Blue - #2820 Robin Egg
Green - #2615 Lt Celery
Red - #2919 Barn Red
Gold - #2327 Sandstone
Brown - #2368 Dk Brown
White - #2101 White

WESTINGHOUSE
Lion Brand® Vanna's Choice®
Lt Brown - #124 Toffee
Green - #174 Olive
Brown - #126 Chocolate
Tan - #123 Beige
Dk Brown - #127 Espresso
TLC® Essentials™
Red - #2919 Barn Red
Lion Brand® Fun Fur
Rust - #134 Copper

SHALIMAR
Bernat® Berella® "4®"
Black - #08994 Black
Bernat® Baby Bouclé
White - #00101 Soft White